The Story of a Special Day
Volume 68

March 8

67th day of the year
(68th in leap years)
298 days remaining
until the end of the year.

by Michael Dobson

Timespinner
Press

For more information about the series, about me, or about your special day, please email us at editor@timespinnerpress.com.

Look for other volumes in *The Story of a Special Day,* coming often.

Table of Contents

Cover: Detail from a poster for International Women's Day, March 8, 1914.

March 8 Quotations

"A word is not a crystal, transparent and unchanging, it is the skin of a living thought and may vary greatly in colour and content according to the circumstances and time in which it is used."

— *Justice Oliver Wendell Holmes Jr., born March 8, 1841*

"There is nothing — absolutely nothing — half so much worth doing as simply messing about in boats."

— *Kenneth Grahame, born March 8, 1859*

"A definition is the start of an argument, not the end of one."

— *Neil Postman, born March 8, 1931*

"The cynic is one who never sees a good quality in a man and never fails to see a bad one."

— *Henry Ward Beecher, died March 8, 1887*

International Women's Day

International Women's Day (IWD), celebrated each year on March 8, began as a political movement associated with the struggle for women's suffrage. In some countries, the celebration is strongly associated with political and human rights. Elsewhere, International Women's Day is a more general celebration of women, a mix of Mother's Day and Valentine's Day. In either form, IWD is celebrated in over 100 nations each March 8.

The struggle to achive women's suffrage, the right of women to vote, was slow to get started. Some women (primarily property owners) had a limited right to vote in Sweden, the Pitcairn Islands, and Sierra Leone. One woman in the Massachusetts Colony voted in the mid-1700s. However, it wasn't until the turn of the 20th century that the struggle for women's suffrage became widespread.

Like other then-radical ideas like labor unions and civil rights, women's suffrage was often associated with political movements on the left. The Socialist Party of America first observed a Women's Day in February 1909, and the following year at an international socialist conference, the idea of the IWD was formalized, and over a million people in Austria, Denmark, Germany, and Switzerland celebrated the holiday in 1911.

In 1914, the official date of IWD was established as March 8. Three years later, International Women's Day in Russia set off the February Revolution, leading to the abdication of Tsar Nicholas II. The Soviet Union declared IWD a national holiday, and for many years, it was primarily celebrated in communist and socialist nations.

In 1977, the United Nations General Assembly proclaimed March 8 as the UN Day for women's rights and world peace, and IWD is now recognized in countries throughout the world. In 2011, President Barack Obama declared March to be "Women's History Month" in honor of the hundredth anniversary of the first IWD.

Heraus mit dem Frauenwahlrecht

FRAUEN-TAG!

8. MÄRZ 1914

Den Frauen, die als Arbeiterinnen, Mütter und Gemeindebürgerinnen ihre volle Pflicht erfüllen, die im Staat wie in der Gemeinde ihre Steuern entrichten müssen, hat Voreingenommenheit und reaktionäre Gesinnung das volle Staatsbürgerrecht bis jetzt verweigert.

Dieses natürliche Menschenrecht zu erkämpfen, muß der unerschütterliche, feste Wille jeder Frau, jeder Arbeiterin sein. Hier darf es kein Ruhen kein Rasten geben. Kommt daher alle, ihr Frauen und Mädchen in die am

Sonntag den 8. März 1914 nachmittags 3 Uhr stattfindenden

9 öffentl. Frauen-Versammlungen

Poster for International
Women's Day, March 8, 1914

5

March 8 Holidays and Celebrations

Revolution Day (Syria)

In Syria, March 8 is known as ثورة الثامن من اذار (Ṭaurät aṯ-Ṯāmin min Āḏār). It celebrates the 1963 Syrian coup d'état that brought the Arab Socialist Ba'ath Party to power.

Women of Aviation Worldwide Week

Women of Aviation Worldwide Week is held each year during the week that includes March 8, commemorating both International Women's Day and also the issuance of the first pilot's license to a woman in 1910 (see "What Happened on March 8?")

Christian Feast Days

Saints commemorated on March 8 include John of God (March 8, 1495 — March 8, 1550) and Saint Philemon of Antinoë.

What Happened on March 8?

1985 CE - Beirut Car Bombing

In an attack allegedly organized by the CIA and British intelligence, a car bomb exploded near the house of Shi'a cleric السيد محمد حسين فضل الله (Grand Ayatollah Sayyid Muhammad Hussein Fadl-Allāh), often referred to as the "spiritual mentor" of the Lebanese militant group Hezbollah. The explosion killed 80 people and wounded 256, many of them women worshippers leaving Friday prayers at a nearby mosque. The intended target escaped without injury. The CIA denied involvement, and Fadl-Allāh denied any role with Hezbollah.

1983 CE - Ronald Reagan Calls the Soviet Union an "Evil Empire"

In a speech before the National Association of Evangelicals in Orlando, Florida, Ronald Reagan made his first recorded use of the phrase "evil empire" in referring to the Soviet Union.

Ronald Reagan delivering the "Evil Empire" speech

1979 CE - The Compact Disc is Introduced

On Mrch 8, 1979, the Philips Corporation, in a press conference in Eindhoven, Netherlands, gave the first public demonstration of an optical digital audio disc, establishing the technical standard used by other manufacturers. Although both Philips and Sony had been developing prototypes for some time, Philips was first to reach the public, with Sony presenting their disc five days later.

1978 CE - First Broadcast of "The Hitchhiker's Guide to the Galaxy"

Douglas Adams' radio series "The Hitchhiker's Guide to the Galaxy" was first broadcast on BBC Radio 4 on Wednesday, March 8, 1978. It quickly grew into a cult classic, spawning books, movies, stage shows, TV series, computer games, and comic book adaptations.

1974 CE - Charles de Gaulle Airport Opens

On March 8, 1974, France's largest airport, Aéroport Paris-Charles de Gaulle (CDG) opened. It is the sixth busiest passenger airport in the world and the second busiest in Europe, and is the principal hub for Air France.

1966 CE - Nelson Pillar Bombing

The Nelson Pillar, a monument to Horatio Nelson in Dublin, Ireland, built in 1809, was destroyed in a bomb blast by a group of former

Irish Republican Army volunteers. No one was killed. The Pillar, which had long been controversial in Dublin, was replaced by a new monument, the Spire of Dublin.

1963 CE - 8 March Revolution in Syria

On March 8, 1963, tanks and units loyal to the Ba'ath Party, an Arab nationalist movement that had already seized power in next-door Iraq, seized critical military and communications facilities in Damascus, and declared a new government. Coincidentally, March 8 was also the anniversary of the founding of the Kingdom of Syria in 1920.

1957 CE - Georgia Memorial to Congress

In an attempt to maintain the institution of segregation, the Georgia legislature passed a resolution asking the U.S. Congress to declare the 14th and 15th Amendments to the Constitution null and void. The bill, known as the "Georgia Memorial to Congress," was signed by the governor of Georgia on March 8, 1957, and was ignored by Congress upon its receipt.

1937 CE - Battle of Guadalajara

The Spanish Civil War, a conflict between the established republican government and the rebel Nationalists, led by future dictator General Francisco Franco, raged from 1936 to 1939. The Nationalists, allied with the Italian Fascist government, tried to encircle and capture the capital city of Madrid. This battle, known as the Battle of Guadalajara, began on March 8, 1937, and would continue until March 23, ending with success for the Republican People's Army. This was, alas, the last major victory of the army, and the Spanish Republic came to an end two years later.

Battle of Guadalajara

1924 CE - Castle Gate Mine Disaster

On March 8, 1924, three explosions ripped through the Utah Fuel Company's Castle Gate Mine #2, killing all 171 men working in the mine. The explosions were later determined to have been caused by a failure to properly dampen coal dust in the mine during the previous shift. It currently ranks as the 10th worst mining disaster in U.S. history.

1916 CE - Battle of Dujaila

On March 8, 1916, as part of World War I, Ottoman forces were besieging the town of Kut, in present-day Iraq, when a British-Indian relief force tried to relieve Kut. Although the British Empire forces numbered nearly 20,000, against an Ottoman force half the size, the British failed, losing 3,500 men to 1,200 on the Ottoman side.

1910 CE - First Female Pilot License

Pioneering French aviatrix Raymonde de Laroche became the first woman to receive a pilot's license on March 8, 1910. She was given licence #36 of the Fédération Aéronautique Internationale. Women of Aviation Worldwide Week is held annually to mark this anniversary.

Raymonde de Laroche in her Voisin biplane, 1910

1868 CE - Sakai Incident (堺事件)

On March 8, 1868, 11 French sailors from the corvette *Dupleix* landed in the port of Sakai, near Osaka, Japan. Because at the time the port of Sakai was not open to foreign ships, samurai of the Tosa clan attacked and killed the sailors. After the French captain protested, the Sakai government paid an indemnity of $150,000, and agreed to execute 20 samurai. In protest, 11 of the samurai committed *seppuku*, or ritual disembowelment, in front of the shocked French, who requested the remaining samurai be banished instead of executed.

Illustration of the Sakai Incident from *Le Monde Illustré*, 1868.

1817 CE - New York Stock Exchange Established

On March 8, 1817, a previously informal group of stockbrokers established the "New York Stock & Exchange Board." It is now the world's largest stock exchange by market capitalization of its listed companies, over $14 trillion as of 2011.

1782 CE - Gnadenhütten Massacre

On March 8, 1782, during the American Revolutionary War, 96 Native Americans of the Lenape (Delaware) tribe who had converted to Christianity were killed by Pennsylvania colonial militia at the Moravian missionary village of Gnadenhütten, Ohio, in revenge for raids made by Native Americans of other unrelated tribes. The site of the massacre is listed on the National Register of Historic Places.

1722 CE - Battle of Gulnabad

On Sunday, March 8, 1722, a battle between Afghani forces and the Safavid Empire of Iran ended in the defeat and fall of the Safavid dynasty.

Portrait of Queen Anne by Michael Dahl, 1705.

16

1702 CE - Queen Anne Takes the Throne

On March 8, 1702, Queen Anne became monarch of England, Scotland, and Ireland, succeeding William and Mary. Although she became pregnant 17 times, she died without any surviving children, and was thus the last monarch of the House of Stuart.

1655 CE - First American Slave for Life

In 1653, John Casor, a black man, sued for his freedom on the grounds that as an indentured servant, he was entitled to freedom after a period of seven years. The Northampton County (Virginia) court ruled against him, making him the first American officially declared a slave.

1618 CE - Kepler's Third Law

After some twelve years of research and observation of the movements of the planets following his discovery of the first two Laws of Planetary Motion, astronomer Johannes Kepler discovered what became known as his Third Law of Planetary Motion: the proportion between the periodic times of any two planets is precisely 1-1/2 times the proportion of the mean distances.

Who Was Born on March 8?

The abbreviation "O.S." on some dates refers to the fact that the Russian Empire did not switch from the Julian to the Gregorian calendar at the same time as the rest of Europe, and therefore some figures have two dates for their birth or death.

People whose original names are not in the Western alphabet have their native names in the appropriate script shown in parenthesis. These characters may not display on all devices.

Acting and Film

James Van Der Beek (March 8, 1977 —)

Actor James Van Der Beek came to fame for portraying Dawson Leery in the WB series *Dawson's Creek* and for playing a fictionalized version of himself in the ABC sitcom *Don't Trust the B— in Apartment 23.*

Freddie Prinze, Jr. (March 8, 1976 —)

Freddie Prinze Jr. first came to fame starring in the 1997 film *I Know What You Did Last Summer*, and has appeared in numerous other films and television shows. He is married to *Buffy the Vampire Slayer* star Sarah Michelle Gellar.

Boris Kodjoe (March 8, 1973 —)

Austrian-born actor Boris Kodjoe appeared in the Showtime series *Soul Food* and the NBC series *Undercovers,* along with movie roles.

Camryn Manheim (March 8, 1961 —)

Actress Camryn Manheim earned Golden Globe and Emmy nominations for playing the mother of Elvis Presley in the 2005 mini-series *Elvis,* and has appeared in featured roles in numerous TV series and films.

Aidan Quinn (March 8, 1959 —)

Aidan Quinn has received two Emmy nominations for his numerous television and film roles.

Lynn Redgrave (March 8, 1943 — May 2, 2010)

Actress Lynn Redgrave came to fame in such films as 1963's *Tom Jones* and 1966's *Georgy Girl,* winning an Oscar nomination for the latter role.

Susan Clark (March 8, 1940 —)

Susan Clark is best known for playing the mother on the sitcom *Webster.*

Sue Ane Langdon (March 8, 1936 —)

Actress Sue Ane Langdon appeared in two Elvis Presley movies and won a Golden Globe for her role in the CBS television series *Arnie.*

Sue Ane Langdon

Gerald Potterton (March 8, 1931 —)

Director and animator Gerald Potterton is best known for his animation work on *Yellow Submarine* and for directing the 1981 animated film *Heavy Metal.*

Cyd Charisse (March 8, 1922 — June 17, 2008)

Actress and dancer Cyd Charisse starred with Fred Astaire and Gene Kelly in such films as *Singin' in thr Rain, The Band Wagon,* and *Silk Stockings.* She received the National Medal of the Arts and Humanities in 2006.

Alan Hale, Jr. (March 8, 1918 — January 2, 1990)

Actor Alan Hale, Jr., is best known for playing the Skipper on the long-running sitcom *Gilligan's Island.*

Alan Hale, Jr.

Claire Trevor (March 8, 1910 — April 8, 2000)

Known as the "Queen of Film Noir" for various "bad girl" roles, Claire Trevor won the Academy Award for Best Supporting Actress for her role in 1948's *Key Largo*.

Louise Beavers (March 8, 1902 — October 26, 1962)

African-American actress Louise Beavers was well known in the 1920s and 1930s as the symbol of the "mammy archetype" in the movies, with roles in over 150 films. She was inducted into the Black Filmmakers Hall of Fame in 1976.

Louise Beavers (left) with Carole Lombard in
1939's *Made For Each Other*

Art and Graphics

Frederick Goudy (**March 8, 1865 — May 11, 1947**)

American type designer Frederick Goudy is known for his typefaces Copperplate Gothic, Kennerly, and Goudy Old Style.

Goudy Old Style

Aa Qq Rr

Aa Qq Rr

Adirondacks

abcdefghijklm
nopqrstuvwxyz
0123456789

Colin Campbell Cooper (March 8, 1856 — November 6, 1937)

American Impressionist painter Colin Cooper is best known for his architectural paintings of New York City skyscrapers.

Rooftops at Sunset, Colin Campbell Cooper, 1912

Crime

Mohammed Bouyeri (محمد بويري)
(March 8, 1978 —)

Islamist Dutch convicted murderer Mohammed Bouyeri is serving a life sentence without parole for the assassination of Dutch film director Theo van Gogh.

Music

Kristinia DeBarge (March 8, 1990 —)

Appearing on the *American Idol* spinoff *American Juniors* in 2003, Kristinia DeBarge reached the top 20 with her first pop single, "Goodbye" in 2009.

Cheryl "Salt" James (March 8, 1966 —)

Rapper and actress Cheryl James is "Salt" in the rap trio Salt-n-Pepa.

Gary Numan (March 8, 1958 —)

Pioneer electronic music performer Gary Numan topped the charts in 1979 with "Are 'Friends' Electric?" and "Cars."

Peggy March (March 8, 1988 —)

Pop singer Peggy March is best known for her 1963 chart-topper "I Will Follow Him."

Carol Bayer Sager (March 8, 1947 —)

Pop composer Carol Bayer Sager wrote numerous hits beginning with "A Groovy Kind of Love," including "Arthur's Theme (Best That You Can Do" and "That's What Friends Are For," many written with her husband Burt Bacharach.

Mike Alsup (March 8, 1947 —)

Guitarist Mike Alsup is best known as a member of the rock group Three Dog Night.

Randy Meisner (March 8, 1946 —)

Bass player and vocalist Randy Meisner was a founding member of the rock groups Poco and The Eagles.

Mickey Dolenz (March 8, 1945 —)

Mickey Dolenz is best known as the drummer and lead vocalist for The Monkees.

The Monkees (left to right): Peter Tork,
Mickey Dolenz, Davy Jones, Mike Nesmith

Pepe Romero (March 8, 1944 —)

Pepe Romero is a world-renowned classical and flamenco guitarist who has recorded over 50 solo albums.

Gábor Szabó (March 8, 1936 — February 26, 1982)

Hungarian jazz guitarist Gábor Szabó is known for his jazz fusion albums and for composing "Gypsy Queen," which became a 1970 Santana hit.

Mississippi John Hurt (March 8, 1893 — November 2, 1966)

Pioneering country blues singer and guitarist Mississippi John Hurt helped trigger the American folk music revival, and influenced musicians including Bob Dylan, Jerry Garcia, Doc Watson, and Taj Mahal.

Mississippi John Hurt

Politics, Law and Military

George Allen (March 8, 1952 —)

Former US senator and governor of Virginia, George Allen lost re-election to the Senate in 2006 for referring to an opposing staffer with the racial epithet "macaca."

Pete Dawkins (March 8, 1938 —)

Former Heisman Trophy winner Pete Dawkins was a Rhodes Scholar, an Army General, unsuccessful Senate candidate, and vice-chairman of Citigroup Private Bank.

Juvénal Habyarimana (March 8, 1937 — April 6, 1994)

President of Rwanda for twenty years, Juvénal Habyarimana supported the Hutu against the Tutsi. Called a dictator by his critics, Habyarimana was assassinated in 1994. His death helped spark the Rwandan Genocide.

Jennings Randolph (March 8, 1902 — May 8, 1998)

West Virginia senator Jennings Randolph is known for his sponsorship of the 26th Amendment, which granted 18-year olds the right to vote.

Oliver Wendell Holmes, Jr. (March 8, 1841 — March 6, 1935)

Associate Supreme Court Justice Oliver Wendell Holmes, Jr., is one of the most cited American legal scholars of the 20th century.

Associate Supreme Court Justice Oliver Wendell Holmes, Jr.

Pirates

Anne Bonny (March 8, 1702 — April 2, 1782)

Anne Bonny was the best-known female pirate of the Caribbean. As part of the crew of the *Revenge,* she captured numerous ships and accumulated substantial treasure. She was captured in 1720, but was smuggled out of prison and died many years later.

Anne Bonny

Public Figures

Kat Von D (March 8, 1982 —)

Mexican-American tattoo artist appeared for four seasons on the TLC reality television show *LA Ink*.

Kim Ung-yong (김웅용) (March 8, 1963 —)

Child prodigy Kim Ung-yong was listed in the Guiness Book of World Records under "Highest IQ," with a score of approximately 210. He got his first Ph.D. at the age of 15 and currently works as a civil engineer and professor.

Evelyn Ay Sempier (March 8, 1933 — October 18, 2008)

Evelyn Ay Sempier won the 1954 Miss America pageant. She is the namesake of the Evelyn Ay Sempier Quality of Life Award, given to Miss America contestants involved with the Children' Miracle Network.

Religion

John of God (March 8, 1495 — March 8, 1550)

Friar and saint John of God is one of Spain's leading religious figures. Canonized in 1690, John of God was named the patron saint of

hospitals, the sick, nurses, firefighters, alcoholics, and booksellers. His feast day is March 8, the date of both his birth and his death.

John of God saving a patient from a hospital fire, by Manuel Gómez-Moreno Gonzáles, 1880

Science and Technology

Georges Charpak (March 8, 1924 [incorrectly listed on some official documents as August 1, 1924] — September 29, 2010)

French physicist Georges Charpak won the 1992 Nobel Prize in Physics for his work in the development of improved particle detectors.

Ralph H. Baer (March 8, 1922 —)

Known as the "Father of Video Games," inventor and engineeer Ralph Baer received the National Medal of Technology for inventing the home video game console. He is also known as the inventor of the popular electronic pattern-matching game *Simon*.

John W. Seybold (March 8, 1916 — March 14, 2004)

John W. Seybold is known as the father of computer typesetting, and later founded a series of newsletters and conferences to promote the use of digital technologies.

Howard Aiken (March 8, 1900 — March 14, 1973)

Computing pioneer Howard Aiken was the conceptual designer of IBM's Harvard Mark I computer. He received the prestigious Edison Medal in 1970.

Elmer Keith (March 8, 1899 — February 12, 1984)

Firearms enthusiast Elmer Keith played a key role in the development of the .357 Magnum.

Edward Calvin Kendall (March 8, 1886 — May 4, 1972)

American chemist Edward Kendall shared the 1950 Nobel Prize for Physiology or Medicine for his work on the hormones of the adrenal gland.

Otto Hahn (March 8, 1879 — July 28, 1968)

German chemist Otto Hahn is known as the "father of nuclear chemistry." He won the 1944 Nobel Prize in Chemistry among numerous other honors, and fought against Jewish persecution by the Nazi government at great personal risk during World War II.

Otto Hahn (right) with physicist Lise Meitner, 1913

Alvan Clark (March 8, 1804 — August 19, 1887)

Telescope lens maker Alvan Clark made the telescopes for the U. S. Naval Observatory, the Lick Observatory, and the Yerkes Observatory, the latter of which is the largest refracting telescope in the world.

Telescope at Yerkes Observatory

Sports

Petra Kvitová (March 8, 1990 —)

Czech professional tennis player Petra Kvitová was ranked #2 in the world in 2011, one of only three players to reach the WTA Championships in her first attempt.

Armanti Edwards (March 8, 1988 —)

Appalachian State quarterback Armanti Edwards was the first back-to-back and two-time winner of the Walter Payton Award for Most Outstanding Offensive Player. He was drafted by the Carolina Panthers in 2010.

Hines Ward (March 8, 1976 —)

Wide receiver Hines Ward was voted MVP of Superbowl XL while playing 14 seasons with the Pittsburgh Steelers.

Jason Elam (March 8, 1970 —)

Denver Bronco Jason Elam is tied for the longest field goal in NFL history: 63 yards.

Buck Williams (March 8, 1960 —)

NBA star Buck Williams ranks 13th in all-time career rebounds, and received numerous honors in his 18 year professional career.

David Wilkie (March 8, 1954 —)

Scottish Sports Hall of Fame swimmer David Wilkie won a gold and two silver medals in the Olympics in 1972 and 1976.

Jim Rice (March 8, 1953 —)

Boston Red Sox left fielder Jim Rice was an eight-time American League All-Star and MVP in 1978. He was inducted into the Baseball Hall of Fame in 2009.

Natalia Kuchinskaya (Наталья Кучинская) (March 8, 1949 —)

Soviet gymnast Natalia Kuchinskaya won two gold medals and two bronze medals in the 1968 Olympics.

Natalia Kuchinskaya, 1966

Ann Packer (March 8, 1942 —)

British track and field athlete Ann Packer won a gold and a silver medal in the 1964 Tokyo Olympics.

Dick Allen (March 8, 1942 —)

Baseball player and R&B singer Dick Allen won Rookie of the Year in 1964, and was named American League MVP in 1972. He is considered the second-most controversial player in baseball history, behind Rogers Hornsby.

Lidiya Skoblikova (Лидия Павловна Скобликова) (March 8, 1939 —)

Soviet speed skater Lidiya Skoblikova won six Olympic gold medals and 25 World Championship gold medals.

Jim Bouton (March 8, 1939 —)

Former MLB pitcher Jim Bolton is the author of the controversial baseball book *Ball Four.*

Hans Fogh (March 8, 1938 —)

Competitive sailor Hans Fogh won two Olympic medals and numerous world and European championships, and was named to the Canada Sports Hall of Fame.

Carl Furillo (March 8, 1922 — January 21, 1989)

Dodger right fielder Carl Furillo batted over .300 five times and was a member of seven National League championship teams from 1947 to 1959.

Words

Richard Fariña (March 8, 1937 — April 30, 1966)

Folksinger and writer Richard Fariña is best known for his 1966 novel *Been Down So Long It Looks Like Up To Me.*

Neil Postman (March 8, 1931 — October 5, 2003)

Cultural critic Neil Postman is best known for his 1985 book about television, *Amusing Ourselves to Death.*

Warren Bennis (March 8, 1925 —)

Organizational consultant and author Warren Bennis is recognized as a pioneer in the field of leadership studies, and is the author of 30 books.

Kenneth Grahame (March 8, 1859 — July 6, 1932)

Scottish author Kenneth Grahame is best known for his 1908 children's classic *The Wind in the Willows*.

Cover of *The Wind in the Willows,* by Kenneth Grahame

Who Died on March 8?

Acting and Film

Robert Pastorelli (June 21, 1954— March 8, 2004)

Robert Pastorelli is known for his role as the house painter on the TV series *Murphy Brown* and as a hit man in the 2005 *Be Cool,* released after his death from a heroin overdose.

Edward Winter (June 3, 1937 — March 8, 2001)

Actor Edward Winter is best known for his recurring role as Colonel Flagg on the long-running television series *M*A*S*H.*

Peggy Cass (May 21, 1924 — March 8, 1999)

Actress Peggy Cass won a Tony Award and an Oscar nomination for her role in the stage and film versions of *Auntie Mame,* but is perhaps best known as a panelist on the long-running TV game show *To Tell the Truth.*

George Stevens (December 18, 1904 — March 8, 1975)

Director George Stevens' notable films include *The Diary of Anne Frank, Giant, Shane,* and *A Place in the Sun,* receiving two Academy Awards for his direction.

Harold Lloyd (April 20, 1893 — March 8, 1971)

One of the most popular film comedians of the silent era, Harold Lloyd made nearly 200 films. He is best known for the iconic image in which he hangs from the hands of a clock high above the street.

Harold Lloyd in the 1928 film *Safety Last.*

Animals

Hachikō (ハチ公) (November 10, 1923—March 8, 1935)

During his owner's life, the Akita dog Hachikō met him every day after work at the railway station. After his owner's death, the dog continued to show up faithfully on time every day for the next nine years, becoming a national symbol throughout Japan for his fidelity. His stuffed and mounted remains are displayed at the National Science Museum of Japan, and statues of the dog can be found in several locations throughout the country.

Hachikō at the
National Science Museum of Japan

Chess

José Raúl Capablanca (November 19, 1888 — March 8, 1942)

Cuban chess grandmaster José Capablanca is regarded as one of the greatest and most naturally talented players in chess history. He was world chess champion from 1921 to 1927.

Crime

William Poole (July 24, 1821 — March 8, 1855)

Bare-knuckle boxer William "Bill the Butcher" Poole was a member of the New York Bowery Boys gang and a leader in the Know-Nothing political movement. He died in a bare-knuckle bout with his archenemy John Morrissey, a Tammany Hall enforcer. He was the inspiration for Daniel Day-Lewis's character in Martin Scorsese's 2002 film *Gangs of New York.*

Literature

Sherwood Anderson (September 13, 1876 — March 8, 1941)

Novelist and short story writer Sherwood Anderson is best known for his work *Winesburg, Ohio*. He helped William Faulkner and Ernest Hemingway get published.

Magic

Ali Bongo (December 8, 1929 — March 8, 2009)

British comedy magician Ali Bongo (William Oliver Wallace) performed as the "Shriek of Araby." A "magician's magician," he consulted on numerous magic programs and served as president of The Magic Circle.

Medicine

Sir Brian Gerald Barratt-Boyes (January 13, 1924 — March 8, 2006)

Pioneering heart surgeon Brian Barratt-Boyes made numerous breakthroughs in his field, and co-wrote the standard reference work *Cardiac Surgery*.

Music

Hank Locklin (February 15, 1918 — March 8, 2009)

A member of the Grand Ole Opry for 50 years, country star Hank Locklin's hits included "Please Help Me, I'm Falling" and "Send Me the Pillow That You Dream On."

Adam Faith (June 23, 1940 — March 8, 2003)

British teen idol Adam Faith was the first UK artist to reach the Top 5 with his first seven hits.

Billy Eckstine (July 8, 1914 — March 8, 1993)

Swing-era balladeer and bandleader Billy Eckstine led the original bop big band and was the first romantic black male in American popular music. His 1948 single "I Apologize" received the Grammy Hall of Fame Award in 1999.

Billy Eckstine

Ron "Pigpen" McKernan (September 8, 1945 — March 8, 1973)

Founding member of the Grateful Dead, Pigpen was inducted into the Rock and Roll Hall of Fame in 1994 along with his fellow bandmembers.

Hector Berlioz (December 11, 1803 — March 8, 1869)

Romantic composer Hector Berlioz is known for his 1830 *Symphonie fantastique* and his 1839 *Roméo et Juliette*.

Politics, Law and Military

Abū ʿAbbās (ابو عباس) (December 10, 1948 — March 8, 2004)

Founder of the Palestine Liberation Front (PLF), Abū ʿAbbās is infamous for his leadership of the 1985 *Achille Lauro* hijacking.

"Mad Jack" Churchill (September 16, 1906 — March 8, 1996)

British lieutenant colonel Jack Churchill fought throughout World War II armed with a longbow and a Scottish broadsword. His motto was "Any officer who goes into action without his sword is improperly armed."

Jack Churchill (right) with sword leading the charge

Edward Terry Sanford (July 23, 1865 — March 8, 1930)

Associate Supreme Court Justice Edward Terry Sanford served on the court from 1923 to 1930.

William Howard Taft (September 15, 1857 — March 8, 1930)

William Howard Taft was the 27th President of the United States and afterward the 10th Chief Justice of the Supreme Court, the only person to have held both offices.

William Howard Taft

Millard Fillmore (January 7, 1800 — March 8, 1874)

Millard Fillmore was the 13th president of the United States. A pro-slavery president, he was active in the Know-Nothing political movement and is ranked in the bottom ten of historical rankings of U.S. presidents.

Benjamin Ruggles Woodbridge (March 5, 1739 — March 8, 1819)

A colonel in the Massachusetts militia during the American Revolutionary War, Woodbridge was a commander at the Battle of Bunker Hill and served in other Revolutionary battles.

William III of England (November 5, 1650 — March 8, 1702)

Dutch stadtholder William of Orange became King of England after the Glorious Revolution of

1688. Reigning with his wife Mary II, their joint reign is often referred to as "William and Mary."

Portrait of Mary II and William III of England

Religion

Henry Ward Beecher (June 24, 1813 — March 8, 1887)

Clergyman, social reformer and abolitionist Henry Ward Beecher crusaded against slavery. In 1875, he was caught up in the Beecher-Tilton affair, one of the most notorious American trials of the 19th century.

Henry Ward Beecher

John of God (March 8, 1495 — March 8, 1550)

Saint John of God, who was born and died on March 8, is covered in the "Who Was Born on March 8?" section of this book.

Science and Technology

César Lattes (July 11, 1924 — March 8, 2005)

Brazilian experimental physicist César Lattes discovered the pion, a composite subatomic particle made up of a quark and an antiquark.

Johannes Diderik van der Waals (November 23, 1837 — March 8, 1923)

Dutch theoretical physicist Johannes van der Waals won the 1910 Nobel Prize in Physics. He is known for the van der Waals equation, the van der Waals forces, van der Waals molecules, and van der Waals radii.

Ferdinand Graf von Zeppelin (July 8, 1838 — March 8, 1917)

Ferdinand von Zeppelin invented the airship (steerable lighter than air) design that bears his name. It consisted of a rigid aluminum frame covered in fabric and containing individual gas cells filled with hydrogen or helium, unlike a blimp, which does not have a rigid frame and consists only of a large envelope of hydrogen or helium. Zeppelins later became popular as passenger vessels until the 1937 Hindenburg disaster along with improvements in heavier-than-air airplanes made them obsolete.

Count von Zeppelin witnesses the landing of one of his airships

John Ericsson (July 31, 1803— March 8, 1889)

Swedish-American inventor and engineer John Ericsson is best known for designing the Civil War ironclad ship *USS Monitor.*

James Buchanan Eads (May 23, 1820 — March 8, 1887)

Civil engineer and inventor James Buchanan Eads produced seven ironclad Civil War ships for the U.S. Navy in only five months, designed the first road and rail bridge to cross the Mississippi (the Eads Bridge in St. Louis), and received over 50 patents in his long and distinguished career.

Sports

Joe DiMaggio (November 25, 1914 — March 8, 1999)

Baseball Hall of Famer "Joltin' Joe" DiMaggio is best known for his 56-game hitting streak in 1941, and for being the second husband of Marilyn Monroe.

Joe DiMaggio, 1937

Ray Nitschke (December 29, 1936— March 8, 1998)

Green Bay Packer middle linebacker Ray Nitschke played from 1958 to 1972, and was named to the Pro Football Hall of Fame. He was also named the NFL's all-time top linebacker.

Howie Morenz (September 21, 1902— March 8, 1937)

Known as the "Stratford Streak," NHL hockey star Howie Morenz was named the best hockey player of the first half of the 20th century.

The month of March, from the illuminated manuscript *Les Très Riches Heures du duc de Berry*

March: The Third Month

In ancient Rome, March was the first month of the year. As the first month of spring, in the Mediterranean climate it marked the beginning of the military campaign season. That's why March (Martius) is named in honor of Mars, the Roman god of war.

Although the first month of the year was moved back to January sometime during the transition of Rome from a kingdom to a republic (historians differ), March was the first month of the year in Russia until the end of the 15th Century, and is the first month of the year in many other cultures and religions.

In the northern hemisphere, March 1 marks the beginning of meteorological spring. In the southern hemisphere, March is the equivalent of September, making southern hemisphere March the beginning of autumn.

March is one of the seven months that have 31 days in it. March starts on the same day of the week as November every year, and except for leap years starts on the same day as February. March starts on the same day of the week as the previous June except for leap years, and in leap years starts on the same day as the previous September and December.

March in Other Cultures

In Finland, March is called *maaliskuu* (earthy month). In Ukraine, it's *березень* (birch tree). Other names for March include *Lentmona*t (Saxon), *Hyld-monath* (Angles), and *sušec* (Slovene).

March Symbols

Birthstones: Aquamarine and bloodstone, both representing courage.

Aquamarine

Birth Flowers Daffodils

Daffodils in Bagatelle Park, Paris, France

March Events

Honorary months: Presidents, Congresses, and nations around the world issue proclamations recognizing particular months to honor certain causes. These events generally fall in March. (All US unless otherwise noted.)

- National Nutrition Month
- American Red Cross Month
- Women's History Month (celebrated in Canada during October)
- Irish-American Heritage Month
- Colorectal Cancer Awareness Month
- Fire Prevention Month (The Philippines)

Women's Suffrage picket line, 1917

"March Madness": (United States) The NCAA Men's Division I Basketball Championship, popularly known as "March Madness" or the "Big Dance," is a single-elimination tournament to establish the champion college basketball team.

Multi-day events: Some March events span multiple days.

- **Nineteen Day Fast:** (Bahá'í Faith) March 2 through March 20

Movable events: Some events change dates from year to year.

- **Commonwealth Day:** Commwealth Day, formerly Empire Day, celebrates the establishment of the Commonwealth of Nations. It is marked by a service in Westminster Abbey and by a speech by England's monarch to the Commonwealht nations around the world. Commonwealth Day is held annually on the second Monday in March, which can fall on any day between March 8 and March 14.

- **Canberra Day:** Canberra Day celebrates the official naming of Australia's capital city. It is also held annually on the second Monday in March.

- **Mardi Gras:** French for "Fat Tuesday," this celebration takes place the day before Ash Wednesday. The New Orleans Mardi Gras celebration is perhaps the most famous, but Mardi Gras and the Carnival season (between Ephiphany and Ash Wednesday) are celebrated in many areas. Mardi Gras can take place between February 3 to March 9 in regular years, to March 10 in leap years.

- **Passion Sunday:** The fifth Sunday of the Christian season of Lent is known as Passion Sunday in various Protestant denominations and by some traditionalist Catholics. Sometimes, the sixth Sunday of Lent is also known as Passion Sunday, but it is more commonly known as Palm Sunday. Passion Sunday starts the two week Passiontide, which ends on Holy Saturday, the day before Easter, commemorating the day that Jesus's body was laid in the tomb.

Mardi Gras Night Parade, New Orleans, 2012

March Zodiac Signs

From the perspective of someone on Earth, the Sun appears to move through the sky throughout the year, along a path astronomers call the ecliptic plane. The ecliptic plane is divided into twelve constellations, known as the zodiac, based on traditionally observed patterns of stars. On your birthday, you can't see your constellation, because it's part of the daytime sky.

The zodiac was first developed by Babylonian astronomers about 2,500 years ago. Because they were unaware that the Earth wobbles like a spinning top (a motion known as *precession*), they didn't make allowance for the fact that the Sun's path through the zodiac changes over time. That means there are now two sets of dates for your birth sign. The *tropical dates* are the original Babylonian dates; the *sidereal dates* tell you where the Sun actually appears as it moves along its annual path.

Zodiac signs for March 8 are Aquarius and Pisces.

Aquarius

Tropical January 20 to February 19

Siderial February 12 to March 8 (March 9 in leap years)

Aquarius is one of the oldest recognized constellations, originally representing the Babylonian god Ea. In Latin, Aquarius means "water-carrier," represented in its symbol. In Greek mythology, Aquarius is sometimes associated with Deucalion, who survived a world-cleansing flood. In Chinese astronomy, it is known as the Black Tortoise of the North (北方玄武, Běi Fāng Xuán Wǔ).

In astrology, Aquarius is considered to be masculine and extroverted, and despite the name is an air sign. Aquarians are supposed to be philanthropical, inventive, and individualistic.

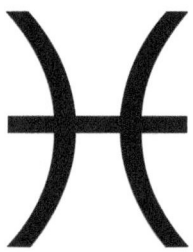

Pisces

Tropical February 20 to March 20

Siderial March 15 to April 14

In the Roman legend of Venus and her son Cupid, they escaped the clutches of Typhon, known as the "father of all monsters," by transforming into fish and tying themselves together with rope. That's why the name Pisces is plural for fish. The constellation appears as a somewhat ragged "V" shape, representing the rope, with the "fish" located at the two rope ends.

In astrology, Pisces is a water sign, compatible with the other water signs Cancer and Scorpio, as well as with the earth signs Taurus, Virgo, and Capricorn. Pisceans are supposed to be imaginative, compassionate, unworldly, secretive, and escapist.

What Day of the Week is March 8?

On what day of the week does March 8 fall?

Surprisingly, this isn't an easy question. Because the calendar year is 365 days long (366 in leap years), it doesn't divide evenly by the seven days of the week.

Also, the Earth goes around the Sun in about 365-1/4 days, so a calendar tends to drift over time. That's why the same date falls on different weekdays in different years.

This is made even more complicated by a change in calendars that took place in 1582. Our modern calendar has its roots in ancient Rome, in a calendar reform conducted by Julius Caesar. Caesar commissioned mathematicians to attack the problem, and came up with the idea of *leap years*, and thus standardized the calendar for centuries to come. This was called the *Julian calendar.*

Over time, however, the small errors in Caesar's calculation compounded. That's why Pope Gregory XIII commissioned the *Gregorian calendar*, used in most of the world today. Some countries converted in 1582, when the calendar was first developed; some converted later; other still haven't changed.

Gregorian and Julian aren't the only types of calendars. The Hebrew year, the Islamic year, and many other calendars are used in different parts of the world and among different people.

You can convert Gregorian dates to other calendars, including the Hebrew calendar, the Islamic calendar, and even the Mayan calendar by visiting the Fourmilab Calendar Converter at http://www.fourmilab.ch/documents/calendar/.

A 50-year brass perpetual calendar.

Copyright, Credit, and Contact

Follow Us

Our blog Dobson's Improbable History features short articles on events and people associated with each day, and updates several times each week. Get the latest on Twitter @SidewiseThinker.

Sources and Art Credits

All art and photographs are either in the public domain or used under a Creative Commons license. Attribution is provided where requested by the copyright owner or when of historical significance, listed below.

- The cover image is a detail from the poster *Frauen Tag*. The full poster is shown with the entry for Women's Day in the "Holidays and Celebrations" chapter of this book. It is in the public domain because its copyright has expired.

- The photograph of Ronald Reagan at the 1983 annual convention of the National Association of Evangelicals is in the public domain because it was taken by an employee of the U.S. Government. It is part of the collection of the U.S. National Archives and Records Administration (ARC identifier 198505).

- The "green smile" illustration from *The Hitchhiker's Guide to the Galaxy* is by Dan Gerhard, and was released into the public domain by the author.

- The photograph from the Battle of Guadalajara was taken by German photographer H. G. von Studnitz and is part of the German Federal Archive (Bundesarchiv, Bild 183-2006-1204-513). It is licensed under the Creative Commons Attribution-Share Alike 3.0 Germany license.

- The photograph of Raymonde de Laroche is from a French postcard in the collection of the Library of Congress (LC-USZ62-107402). It is in the public domain because its copyright has expired.

- The illustration of the Sakai Incident from an 1868 issue of *Le Monde Illustré* is in the public domain because its copyright has expired.

- The 1705 portrait of Anne of Great Britain was painted by Michael Dahl. The original can be seen in the National Portrait Gallery, London. It is in the public domain because its copyright has expired.

- The 1958 publicity photograph of Sue Ane Langdon is in the public domain because it was published between 1923 and 1977 without a copyright notice.

- The publicity photograph of Alan Hale, Jr., is in the public domain because it was published between 1923 and 1977 without a copyright notice.

- The screenshot of Louise Beavers from *Made For Each Other* is in the public domain because it was published between 1923 and 1963 and its copyright was not renewed.

- The specimen of Goudy Old Style typeface is by Jim Hood, and is licensed under the Creative Commons Attribution-Share Alike 3.0 license.

- The 1912 painting *Rooftops at Sunset* by Colin Campbell Cooper is in the public domain because its copyright has expired.

- The 1967 photograph of The Monkees is from a full page trade advertisement for their single, and is in the public domain because it was published between 1923 and 1977 without a copyright notice.

- The 1964 photograph of Mississippi John Hurt at the Library of Congress is in the public domain because it was prepared by an employee of the U.S. government as part of that person's official duties.

- The 1924 photograph of Justice Oliver Wendell Holmes is from the Library of Congress's

National Photo Company collection (LC-F81-33174), and according to the library, there are no known restrictions on the use of this photograph.

- The drawing of pirate Anne Bonny is in the public domain because its copyright has expired.

- The 1880 painting *San Juan de Dios salvando a los enfermos de incendio del Hospital Real* by Manuel Gómez-Moreno Gonzáles is in the public domain because its copyright has expired.

- The 1913 photograph of Lise Meitner and Otto Hahn is from the U.S. Department of Energy,j Office of Public Affairs, and is in the public domain because it was prepared by an employee of the U.S. government as part of that person's official duties.

- The photograph of the 40 inch refractor telescope at Yerkes Observatory was taken by "Kb9vrg" and was released into the public domain by its author.

- The 1966 photograph of gymnast Natalia Kuchinskaya was taken by Ron Kroon, and is part of the Dutch National Archives. It is licensed under the Creative Commons Attribution-Share Alike 3.0 Netherlands license.

- The cover of the 1913 edition of Kenneth Grahame's *The Wind in the Willows* is in the public domain because its copyright has expired.

- The 1928 photograph of Harold Lloyd from the film *Safety Last* is in the public domain because its copyright has expired.

- The photograph of Hachiko in the National Science Museum of Japan is by による撮影, and is licensed under the Creative Commons Attribution ShareAlike 2.1 Japan license.

- The photograph of Billy Eckstine is by William P. Gottlieb, who dedicated the rights to the public domain. It is part of the Library of Congress's William P. Gottlieb collection, DLC 99-401005.

- The photograph of Jack Churchill is from the Imperial War Museum and is in the public domain because its copyright has expired.

- The 1908 photograph of William Howard Taft is from the LIbrary of Congress collection, digital ID cph.3a53300. It is in the public domain because its copyright has expired.

- The detail of William and Mary is from the 18th century Ceiling of the Painted Hall by Sir James Thornhill, and is in the public domain because its copyright has expired.

- The photograph of Henry Ward Beecher is by Thure de Thulstrup, and is part of the Boston Public Library collection. It is in the public domain because its copyright has expired.

- The photograph of the zeppelin landing is from the George Grantham Bain collection, purchased by the Library of Congress (digital ID cph.3a45203) and made available with no known restrictions.

- The 1937 photograph of Joe DiMaggio is from the Harris & Ewing Collection at the Library of Congress (LC-DIG-hec-22989) and there are no known restrictions on the use of this image.

- The illustration of the month of March is from the French Gothic illuminated manuscript *Les Très Riches Heures du duc de Berry* by the Limbourg Brothers, Jean Colombe, and an intermediate painter whose name is lost to history.

- The photograph of aquamarine has been released into the public domain.

- The photograph of daffodils is by Myrabella, and is licensed under the Creative Commons Attribution-Share Alike 3.0 Unported license.

- The 1917 Women's Suffrage demonstration comes from the Library of Congress, Prints and Photographs Division, LC-USZ62-31799 DLC

- The photograph of the 2012 Mardi Gras Night Parade was taken by Mills Baker, licensed under the Creative Commons Attribution 2.0 Generic License. It is cropped for its use in this book.

- The 50-year perpetual calendar photograph is in the public domain.